KT-159-771

When Baby Lost Bunny

For Margaret and John, my big brother and sister,
and our lovely mum! — J.J.

For Daniel Tomos Grace — A.R.

ORCHARD BOOKS
338 Euston Road, London NW1 3BH
Orchard Books Australia
Level 17/207 Kent Street, Sydney, NSW 2000

First published in 2011 by Orchard Books
First published in paperback in 2012

ISBN 978 1 40830 467 9

Text © Julia Jarman 2011
Illustrations © Adrian Reynolds 2011

The rights of Julia Jarman to be identified as the author
and of Adrian Reynolds to be identified as the illustrator
of this book have been asserted by them in accordance
with the Copyright, Designs and Patents Act, 1988.

A CIP catalogue record for this book
is available from the British Library.

10 9 8 7 6 5 4 3 2 1

Printed in China

Orchard Books is a division of Hachette Children's Books,
an Hachette UK company.

www.hachette.co.uk

When Baby Lost Bunny

Julia Jarman   Adrian Reynolds

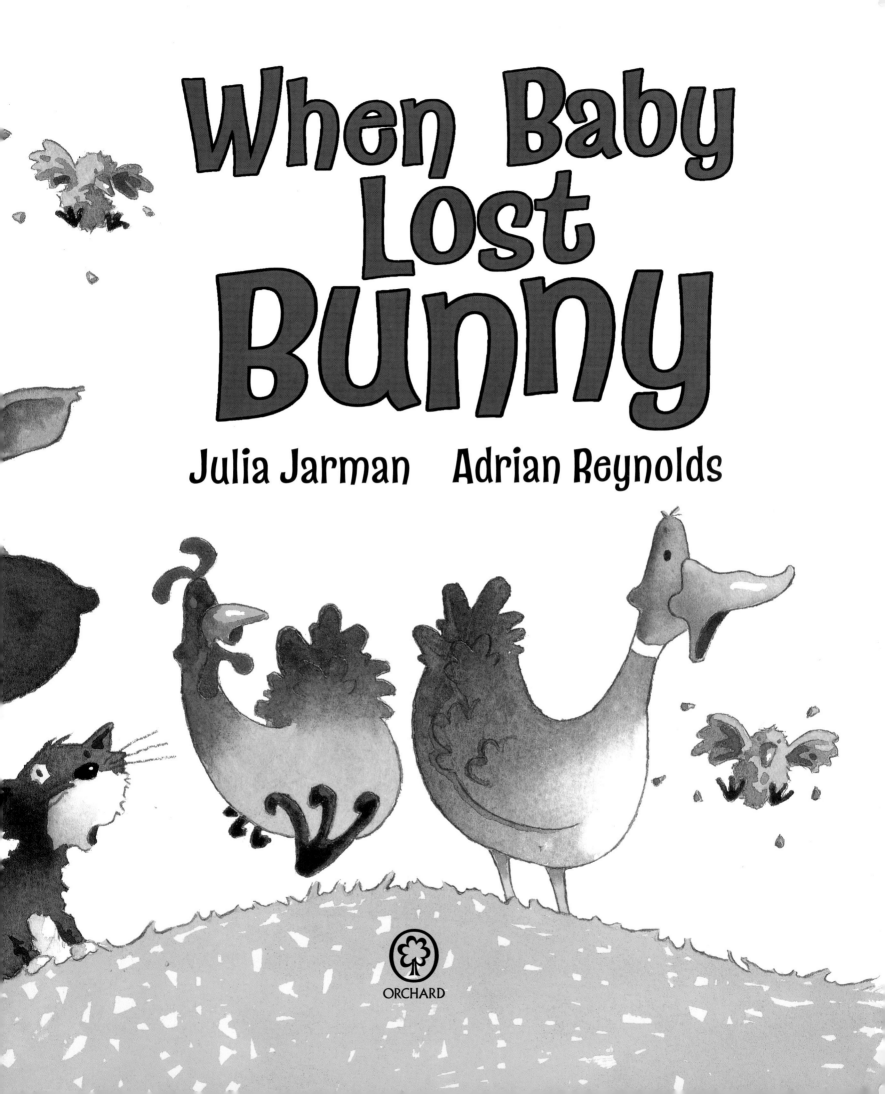

ORCHARD

We went for a walk,
Mummy,

Daddy

and me,

And Baby
in his buggy,

And our dog, Mr D.

Then Baby said, **"Ma!"**

And Mum said, "I'm here!

I'm pushing your buggy.
I'm here, little dear!"

Then we did some more walking,
And Baby said,

"Da!"

And Dad said, "That's me!
Here I am, little star!"

Then,
"Oof-
oof!"

cried Baby,
With his mouth open wide.

"Woof! Woof!"

said our dog.
"Yes, I'm here by your side!"

"Ack-ack!"

shouted Baby.

And Duck said,

"Quack! Quack! Quack!

I'm here, little fellow,
With Hen at the back!"

Then Baby yelled,
"Myoo!"
Ever so loudly.

"Miaow!"

Said Black Cat,
And she followed us proudly.

We carried on walking,
Lots of us now,
And Baby bellowed, **"Ooo!"**

As we passed a cow.

"And 'moo'
to you, Baby!
I'm coming too!"

But Sheep said to Cow,
"Baby didn't say 'Moo!'

Baby said,
'Baa!'
And to me,
not to you."

We all carried on walking,
But Baby started to cry,

"Waa, waa, Waa!"

As tears filled his eyes.
So . . .

Sheep looked at Cow,
Cow looked at Cat,

But none of them knew
What to make of all that.

Cat looked at the chicks,
The chicks looked at Hen,

Hen looked at Duck
Again and again.

Dog looked at Daddy,
Mum shook her head,

"Waa waa!"

But I looked and listened
To what Baby said.

Then, "Back in a minute!"
I started to run
As fast as I could
Back where we'd come.

I looked and I looked
And at last I found . . .

Baby's brown bunny

Alone on the ground!

"He was saying his bunny
Fell down by the gate."

Dad hoisted me high,
"Big Brother,
    you're great!

What would we do
Without you to translate?"

I gave Bunny to Baby,
Who smiled and said,

"Ug!"

So I gave
my little
brother . . .

. . . a big brother hug!